GAO

Report to the Committee on
Oversight and Government Reform
House of Representatives

June 2012

FREEDOM OF INFORMATION ACT

Key Website Is Generally Reliable, but Action Is Needed to Ensure Completeness of Its Reports

GAO
Accountability ★ Integrity ★ Reliability

GAO-12-754

GAO
Accountability * Integrity * Reliability

Highlights

Highlights of GAO-12-754, a report to the Committee on Oversight and Government Reform, House of Representatives

FREEDOM OF INFORMATION ACT

Key Website Is Generally Reliable, but Action Is Needed to Ensure Completeness of Its Reports

Why GAO Did This Study

FOIA establishes a legal right of access to government information on the basis of principles of openness and accountability in government. To facilitate the public's ability to obtain information on federal agencies' compliance with FOIA and other information related to the act, Justice launched a website—FOIA.gov—in March 2011. Accordingly, GAO was requested to determine (1) the origin and reliability of the data on FOIA.gov and (2) the actions being taken to improve FOIA.gov and develop additional capabilities. To accomplish these objectives, GAO reviewed Justice's plan for the website and analyzed the consistency of the data on FOIA.gov and the completeness of the results provided by the website's feature that allows users to create custom reports. GAO also interviewed cognizant Justice and other agency officials.

What GAO Recommends

GAO recommends that Justice ensure that the "Advanced Reporting" feature on FOIA.gov produces reports that are complete. In written comments on a draft of this report, the Director of Justice's Office of Information Policy agreed with GAO's recommendation.

View GAO-12-754. For more information, contact Valerie C. Melvin at (202) 512-6304 or melvinv@gao.gov.

What GAO Found

The Department of Justice's (Justice) website called FOIA.gov presents data from agencies' annual Freedom of Information Act (FOIA) reports. Agencies submit their annual reports to Justice in print and in electronic form and Justice posts the electronic data onto the website. For fiscal year 2010, the data GAO reviewed on the website were generally consistent with the data in the agencies' print versions. According to Justice officials, the department has taken steps to ensure accuracy and consistency of the data. These steps include providing annual training to agency personnel who are responsible for preparation of the FOIA annual reports and posting guidance for report completion and submission on the Office of Information Policy website. In addition, the department has implemented checks to ensure data consistency between the two report versions. Specifically, it has developed and provided agencies with a tool to be used in creating the electronic version for the website. The tool contains features that assist agencies in compiling their data and math checks to help ensure consistency. Further, Justice officials have a checklist they use as a guide for checking the consistency of the electronic versions of agencies' annual reports against the print versions. However, FOIA.gov's "Advanced Reporting" feature, which provides users with the capability to generate custom reports based on user-selected queries, did not always produce complete results. Specifically, certain reports showed data for fewer than the 97 agencies that should have been included. Justice officials stated that they had taken steps to correct the specific instances of incomplete reports that GAO had identified. Nevertheless, GAO's experience in using FOIA.gov raises concerns about whether the website will produce complete reports in response to all queries.

Justice has made improvements to FOIA.gov since the website's initial deployment in March 2011. For example, the department added a search feature to help users locate information on an agency's website, including documents agencies have released in response to previous FOIA requests. Further, in March 2012, the department added information in the Spanish language, as well as links to agencies' FOIA web portals. While Justice does not intend to expand FOIA.gov's capabilities to serve as an internal FOIA processing system, three other agencies—the Environmental Protection Agency, the Department of Commerce, and the National Archives and Records Administration—have undertaken the development of a multiagency system that is intended to complement FOIA.gov and provide such capabilities.

Contents

Abbreviations

Commerce	Department of Commerce
EPA	Environmental Protection Agency
FOIA	Freedom of Information Act
Justice	Department of Justice
NARA	National Archives and Records Administration

GAO
Accountability * Integrity * Reliability

United States Government Accountability Office
Washington, DC 20548

June 28, 2012

The Honorable Darrell Issa
Chairman
The Honorable Elijah Cummings
Ranking Member
Committee on Oversight
  and Government Reform
House of Representatives

The Freedom of Information Act (FOIA)[1] establishes a legal right of access to government information on the basis of principles of openness and accountability in government. FOIA allows the public to request information from federal agencies, which the agencies are required to provide, subject to specified exemptions that allow protection for discrete categories of information.[2] To help ensure accountability, FOIA requires that agencies provide an annual report to the Attorney General; these reports include information as specified in the act, such as how many requests were received and processed in the previous fiscal year, how many requests were pending at the end of the fiscal year, and the median times that agencies or their components took to process the requests.[3] To make the data from agencies' annual FOIA reports more usable (i.e., searchable) and to serve as an educational resource for the public and agencies, the Department of Justice (Justice) launched the website, www.FOIA.gov, in March 2011.

At your request, we conducted a study of the FOIA.gov website. As agreed to with the staff of your committee, our objectives were to determine (1) the origin of the data on FOIA.gov and how reliable are the data and (2) the actions being taken to improve FOIA.gov and develop additional capabilities.

---

[1]5 U.S.C. § 552.

[2]These exemptions permit restrictions on public disclosure for reasons such as protection of personal privacy, national security, and law enforcement.

[3]In an ordered set of values, the median is a value below and above which there is an equal number of values; if there is no one middle number, it is the arithmetic mean (average) of the two middle values.

On April 30, 2012, we provided your offices with briefing slides that outlined the results of our study and we met with your staff to discuss our findings, conclusions, and recommendation. The purpose of this report is to provide the published briefing slides to you and to officially transmit our recommendation to the Department of Justice. The slides, which discuss our scope and methodology, are included in appendix I.

We performed our work in support of this performance audit at the Department of Justice and at the Department of Commerce (Commerce), the Environmental Protection Agency (EPA), and the National Archives and Records Administration (NARA) in Washington, D.C., from October 2011 to April 2012, in accordance with generally accepted government auditing standards. Those standards require that we plan and perform the audit to obtain sufficient, appropriate evidence to provide a reasonable basis for our findings and conclusions based on our audit objectives. We believe that the evidence obtained provides a reasonable basis for our findings and conclusions based on our audit objectives.

In summary, our review highlighted the following:

- The FOIA.gov website presents data that originate in the FOIA annual reports that agencies are required to submit to Justice. The website's fiscal year 2010 data were generally consistent with data that were contained in agencies' published FOIA annual reports. According to officials in the Office of Information Policy, the department has taken steps to ensure the accuracy and consistency of the data. These steps include, but are not limited to, providing annual training to agency personnel who are responsible for preparation of the FOIA annual reports and posting guidance for report completion and submission on the Office of Information Policy website. However, the "Advanced Reporting" feature on FOIA.gov did not always yield reports that were complete. For example, certain reports showed data for fewer than the 97 agencies that should have been included. We discussed these incomplete reports with the Director of the Office of Information Policy and an official from Justice's Chief Information Officer's staff. According to these officials, the department has resolved the incomplete reports we identified. Nonetheless, the incomplete results are cause for concern about whether FOIA.gov will produce complete reports for all queries.

- Justice has made improvements to FOIA.gov since the website's initial deployment in March 2011. For example, the department added a search feature to help users locate information on an agency's website, including documents agencies have released in response to previous FOIA requests. While Justice does not intend to expand FOIA.gov's capabilities to serve as an internal FOIA processing system, EPA, Commerce, and NARA have undertaken development of a multiagency system that is intended to complement FOIA.gov and provide such capabilities.

Conclusions

As intended, the FOIA.gov website is populated with data that originate in the FOIA annual reports that federal agencies are required to submit to Justice. While these data for fiscal year 2010 are generally consistent with those presented in agencies' published annual reports, the website's feature that provides users with the capability to generate customized reports was not reliable because it did not always provide complete results.

Justice has made improvements to enhance FOIA.gov, including the addition of a governmentwide search feature; however, it does not intend for the website to include capabilities that agencies would use to support management of their FOIA processes (e.g., processing FOIA requests). EPA, Commerce, and NARA are currently engaged in a project to develop a multiagency system that is intended to compliment FOIA.gov and provide such capabilities.

Recommendation for Executive Action

To ensure the reliability of reports generated from the "Advanced Reporting" feature of the Department of Justice's website, FOIA.gov, we recommended that the Director of the Office of Information Policy, in conjunction with the department's Chief Information Officer, make certain that the website's "Advanced Reporting" feature produces complete reports in response to all queries.

Agency Comments and Our Evaluation

The Department of Justice provided written comments on a draft of this report, signed by the Director of the Office of Information Policy. In its comments, the department agreed with our recommendation. The Director stated that, while the department's Office of the Chief Information Officer has resolved the issue of some agencies and components of agencies not appearing in certain reports generated by the FOIA.gov advanced reporting feature, the Office of Information Policy, in conjunction with the Office of the Chief Information Officer, will perform additional testing to re-confirm that the FOIA.gov advanced reporting feature is producing complete reports. The Director also noted that, while the department does not intend for FOIA.gov to serve as an internal FOIA processing system for agencies, the website includes features that can assist agencies with their management of FOIA, such as, the ability to compare and contrast their own performance over time and with that of other agencies, assess trends, analyze processing times, and determine whether information responsive to a FOIA request is already publicly available. We agree that these capabilities have the potential to assist agencies in their management of FOIA. The comments are reproduced in appendix II.

Further, we received written comments from the Department of Commerce, signed by the Chief Financial Officer and Assistant Secretary for Administration, and from the National Archives and Records Administration, signed by the Archivist of the United States. These comments are reproduced in appendixes III and IV, respectively. In its comments, Commerce concurred that FOIA.gov is different from, but complimentary to, the multiagency FOIA web portal the department is developing with NARA and EPA. The Archivist commented on the importance of the accuracy and completeness of the data on FOIA.gov. We also requested, but did not receive comments from, the Environmental Protection Agency.

We are sending copies of this report to interested congressional committees. We are also sending copies to the Attorney General; the Director, Office of Information Policy; and other interested parties. Copies of this report will also be available at no charge on GAO's website at http://www.gao.gov.

If you or your staffs have any questions on matters discussed in this report, please contact me at (202) 512-6304 or melvinv@gao.gov. Contact points for our Offices of Congressional Relations and Public Affairs may be found on the last page of this report. GAO staff who made major contributions to this report are listed in appendix II.

Valerie C. Melvin
Valerie C. Melvin
Director
Information Management
   and Technology Resources Issues

GAO
Accountability * Integrity * Reliability

Freedom of Information Act: Key Website Is Generally Reliable, but Action Is Needed to Ensure Completeness of Its Reports

Briefing for the

Committee on Oversight and Government Reform
House of Representatives

April 30, 2012

Appendix I: Briefing for Staff Members of the
Committee on Oversight and Government
Reform, House of Representatives

Briefing Overview

Introduction

Objectives

Scope and Methodology

Results In Brief

Background

Results

   Objective 1

   Objective 2

Conclusions

Recommendation for Executive Action

Agency Comments and Our Evaluation

2

Appendix I: Briefing for Staff Members of the
Committee on Oversight and Government
Reform, House of Representatives

 **Introduction**

The Freedom of Information Act (FOIA)[1] allows the public to request information from federal agencies, which the agencies are required to provide, subject to specified exemptions that allow protection for discrete categories of information.[2] In addition to providing information about government operations and decisions, requests for information through the act have led to disclosure of waste, fraud, abuse, and wrongdoing in the government, as well as the identification of unsafe consumer products, harmful drugs, and serious health hazards. A FOIA request can be made by any person or organization[3] for any agency record.

To help ensure accountability, the act requires that agencies provide an annual report on their FOIA operations to the Attorney General; these reports include information as specified in the act, such as how many requests were received and processed in the previous fiscal year, how many requests were pending at the end of the fiscal year, and the median times that agencies or their components took to process the requests.[4] The Department of Justice launched the website, www.FOIA.gov, in March 2011 to make the data from agencies' annual FOIA reports more usable (e.g., searchable) and to serve as an educational resource for the public and agencies.

---

[1] 5 U.S.C. § 552.

[2] These exemptions permit restrictions on public disclosure for reasons such as protection of personal privacy, national security, and law enforcement.

[3] Any member of the public can make a FOIA request. The request must be in writing and reasonably describe the information sought.

[4] In an ordered set of values, the median is a value below and above which there is an equal number of values; if there is no one middle number, it is the arithmetic mean (average) of the two middle values.

3

Appendix I: Briefing for Staff Members of the
Committee on Oversight and Government
Reform, House of Representatives

Objectives

As agreed to with the Committee staff, our objectives were to determine:

(1) What is the origin of the data on FOIA.gov and how reliable are the data?

(2) What actions, if any, are being taken to improve FOIA.gov and develop additional capabilities?

4

**Appendix I: Briefing for Staff Members of the
Committee on Oversight and Government
Reform, House of Representatives**

 **Scope and Methodology**

To determine the origin of the data on FOIA.gov, we reviewed Justice's plan for the website and interviewed the Director of Justice's Office of Information Policy, who is responsible for the website's content. We then corroborated the official's statements by comparing data on the website with agencies' annual FOIA reports.

To determine the reliability of the data, we analyzed the (1) consistency of the data on FOIA.gov with the data in agencies' published annual reports and (2) completeness of the results provided by the website's feature that allows users to create custom reports.

- To analyze data consistency, we first selected the 15 agencies that received approximately 90 percent of FOIA requests in fiscal year 2010.[5] Further, we selected 16 data fields that represent key FOIA information, including the number of requests, exemptions, appeals, and backlogged requests.[6] We then compared the 240 data elements between FOIA.gov and the agencies' 2010 annual FOIA reports.

---

[5] These agencies were the Departments of Agriculture, Defense, Health and Human Services, Homeland Security, Justice, Labor, State, Transportation, Treasury, Veterans Affairs, and the Environmental Protection Agency, Equal Employment Opportunity Commission, National Archives and Records Administration, Social Security Administration, and the United States Securities and Exchange Commission.

[6] These fields included the Number of Requests Pending as of Start of Fiscal Year, Number of Requests Received, Number of Requests Processed, Number of Requests Pending as of End of Fiscal Year, Number of Full Grants, Number of Partial Grants/Partial Denials, Number of Full Denials based on Exemptions, Number Affirmed on Appeal, Number Partially Affirmed & Partially Reserved/Remanded on Appeal, Number Completely Reserved/Remanded on Appeal, Number of Appeals Closed for Other Reasons, Average Number of Days to Process Simple Requests, Average Number of Days to Process Complex Requests, Average Number of Days to Process Expedited Requests, Total Number of Full Time FOIA Staff, and Total Costs Associated with Handling FOIA Requests.

5

Appendix I: Briefing for Staff Members of the
Committee on Oversight and Government
Reform, House of Representatives

 **G A O**
Accountability · Integrity · Reliability

Scope and Methodology

We did not include agencies' 2008 and 2009 annual FOIA reports in our review because complete data from these years were not available on FOIA.gov.[7] In 2008, 92 agencies were required to submit FOIA reports; in 2009, 94 agencies; in 2010, 97 agencies; and in 2011, 99 agencies. We also met with officials in Justice's Office of Information Policy to discuss their actions to ensure the consistency of data in FOIA.gov with agencies' published 2010 annual FOIA reports. However, our analysis did not include assessing the reliability of the data in agencies' published annual FOIA reports.

- To analyze the completeness of reports produced by FOIA.gov, we generated custom reports using the website's feature that provides users with the capability to create reports. We then checked the reports to ensure that they included data for all the agencies that were represented on FOIA.gov.

To determine the actions being taken to improve FOIA.gov, we interviewed Office of Information Policy officials regarding their recent and planned improvements to the website. We corroborated the officials' statements by accessing FOIA.gov and noting the improvements that were made during the course of our review.

---

[7] According to Justice officials, FOIA.gov does not contain fiscal year 2008 and 2009 data for all agencies because agencies were not required to provide data in the specific open format needed for uploading onto FOIA.gov until fiscal year 2010.

6

Appendix I: Briefing for Staff Members of the
Committee on Oversight and Government
Reform, House of Representatives

Scope and Methodology

To determine actions being taken to develop additional FOIA-related system capabilities, we interviewed officials from the Environmental Protection Agency (EPA), Department of Commerce (Commerce), and the National Archives and Records Administration (NARA) about their planned multiagency FOIA web portal. Additionally, we obtained and reviewed documentation related to the planned web portal, including project plans, requirements documentation, cost documentation, and interagency agreements.

We conducted this performance audit from October 2011 through April 2012 in accordance with generally accepted government auditing standards. Those standards require that we plan and perform the audit to obtain sufficient, appropriate evidence to provide a reasonable basis for our findings and conclusions based on our audit objectives. We believe that the evidence obtained provides a reasonable basis for our findings and conclusions based on our audit objectives.

7

Appendix I: Briefing for Staff Members of the
Committee on Oversight and Government
Reform, House of Representatives

 **G A O**
Accountability · Integrity · Reliability

Results In Brief

The FOIA.gov website presents data that originate in the FOIA annual reports that agencies are required to submit to Justice. The website's fiscal year 2010 data were generally consistent with agencies' published FOIA annual reports. However, FOIA.gov's "Advanced Reporting" feature did not always yield reports that were complete. For example, certain reports showed data for fewer than the 97 agencies that should have been included.

Justice has made improvements to FOIA.gov since the website's initial deployment in March 2011. For example, the department added a search feature to help users locate information on an agency's website, including documents agencies have released in response to previous FOIA requests. While Justice does not intend to expand FOIA.gov's capabilities to serve as an internal FOIA processing system, EPA, Commerce, and NARA have undertaken development of a multiagency system that is intended to complement FOIA.gov and provide such capabilities.

We are recommending that Justice ensure that FOIA.gov's "Advanced Reporting" feature produces complete reports.

An Attorney-Advisor in the Department of Justice, Office of Information Policy submitted written technical comments on a draft of this briefing via e-mail. We have addressed each comment as appropriate. Justice did not provide comments on our conclusions or recommendation.

8

Appendix I: Briefing for Staff Members of the
Committee on Oversight and Government
Reform, House of Representatives

Background

FOIA establishes a legal right of access to government information on the basis of principles of openness and accountability in government. Prior to enactment of the act in 1966, an individual seeking access to federal records had faced the burden of establishing a right to examine them. FOIA established a "right to know" standard, under which an organization or any person could receive access to information held by a federal agency without demonstrating a need or reason. The "right to know" standard shifted the burden of proof from the individual to government agencies and requires agencies to provide proper justification when denying a request for access to a record.

A request for records is the best known FOIA activity, and FOIA requires an agency to promptly provide a record in any readily producible form or format specified by the requester. FOIA also provides the public with access to government information through "affirmative agency disclosure" in which an agency publishes information in the *Federal Register* or on the Internet, including in its electronic "reading room," which is commonly referred to as a FOIA library.

9

Appendix I: Briefing for Staff Members of the
Committee on Oversight and Government
Reform, House of Representatives

 G A O
Accountability · Integrity · Reliability

Background

In 1996, Congress amended FOIA to require each agency to submit a report to the Attorney General on or before February 1 of each year that covers the preceding fiscal year and includes information about the agency's FOIA operations, such as the following:

- number of requests received, processed, and pending at the end of the fiscal year;

- median number of days taken by the agency to process different types of requests;

- number of determinations made by the agency not to disclose information and the reasons for not disclosing the information;

- disposition of administrative appeals by requesters; and

- information on the costs associated with handling FOIA requests and full-time equivalent staffing information.[8]

Justice has lead responsibility for providing guidance and support, including training, to federal agencies on submission of their annual FOIA reports. The Attorney General is required to make the reports from all agencies available online at a single electronic access point and report to Congress no later than April 1 of each year that these reports are available.

---

[8] 5 U.S.C.§ 552(e)(1). Prior to 1996, annual FOIA reports were sent to Congress.

10

Appendix I: Briefing for Staff Members of the
Committee on Oversight and Government
Reform, House of Representatives

Background

The Open Government Directive issued by the Office of Management Budget required that each agency include in their Open Government Plan a specific, new flagship initiative that would address agency transparency, participation, and collaboration.[9] In April 2010, Justice initiated the development of the FOIA.gov website as the flagship initiative under its Open Government Plan to provide greater transparency on agency compliance with FOIA and to serve as an educational resource on how the act works, where to make a request, and what to expect through the FOIA process.[10] According to Justice officials, the website was developed at a cost of about $300,000.[11]

---

[9] Office of Management and Budget, *Memorandum for the Heads of Executive Departments and Agencies – Subject: Open Government Directive,* M-10-06 (Washington, D.C.: Dec. 8, 2009).

[10] Department of Justice, *Open Government Plan,* version 1.1 (Washington, D.C.: June 25, 2010).

[11] According to Justice officials, FOIA.gov was developed in-house by government staff and contractors and was funded through the E-Gov Services Staff operating plan. The officials further stated that the staff and contractors were not strictly dedicated to the FOIA.gov development effort and worked on other tasks besides FOIA.gov.

11

Appendix I: Briefing for Staff Members of the
Committee on Oversight and Government
Reform, House of Representatives

Justice launched FOIA.gov in March 2011. The website allows the public to analyze FOIA activities at the federal agencies required to submit an annual report, track and compare agency FOIA performance, and learn facts about FOIA and how and where to make a request. FOIA.gov also provides the public with access to the detailed data contained in agencies' annual reports and presents the data graphically in charts and tables. The data can be aggregated to show the federal government's FOIA performance, including the number of requests that are received and processed by each agency, the disposition of those requests, and the amount of time taken to respond. The data from the website also allow sorting and comparing of agencies' annual reports over time. The data available on FOIA.gov are limited to fiscal years 2008-2011, with data for future years to be added as they become available.

FOIA.gov is not intended to serve as an internal FOIA processing system for agencies.

See the screenshot in figure 1 for a view of the home page of FOIA.gov.

12

Appendix I: Briefing for Staff Members of the
Committee on Oversight and Government
Reform, House of Representatives

 G A O
Accountability · Integrity · Reliability

Background

Figure 1: Screenshot of the FOIA.gov Website

Source: FOIA.gov web page.

13

Appendix I: Briefing for Staff Members of the
Committee on Oversight and Government
Reform, House of Representatives

 **G A O**
Accountability · Integrity · Reliability

Background

The FOIA.gov website has five tabs a user can choose from to obtain information on agencies' activities: Home, Data, Reports, Find, and Learn.

- Home – briefly describes FOIA, provides links for users to explore FOIA data, provides FOIA data at a glance, highlights significant agency accomplishments based on agencies' annual reports, provides noteworthy reports, and spotlights recent agency disclosures.

- Data – allows generation of reports by selecting from a list of topics (e.g., requests, exemptions, appeals, fee waivers, and backlogs), agencies, and fiscal years.

- Reports – includes links to featured, at-a-glance, most popular, and most recent reports.

- Find – allows searches for information available on all federal government websites.

- Learn – contains information and videos on FOIA, where and how to make a FOIA request, who governs FOIA, frequently asked questions, the administration's policies regarding FOIA, as well as links to other Open Government websites, each federal agency's FOIA website, and FOIA request forms.

14

Appendix I: Briefing for Staff Members of the
Committee on Oversight and Government
Reform, House of Representatives

Background

The website also provides a glossary with commonly used FOIA terms. Further, the website provides a mechanism for soliciting feedback from the public on ways to improve the website.

As of December 2011, FOIA.gov had received almost 2 million page views; the most frequently viewed pages were from the "Data" and "Learn" tabs.

15

Appendix I: Briefing for Staff Members of the
Committee on Oversight and Government
Reform, House of Representatives

FOIA.gov Presents Data That Are Generally Consistent with the Agency FOIA Reports from Which They Originate, but the "Advanced Reporting" Feature Did Not Always Yield Complete Results

Agencies' annual report data on FOIA.gov are generally consistent with their fiscal year 2010 annual reports; however, the "Advanced Reporting" feature did not always provide reports that were complete.

FOIA.gov Is Populated with Agency-Provided Data That Are Generally Consistent with Agencies' FOIA Annual Reports

FOIA requires agencies to annually provide a report on their FOIA activities to the Attorney General. (Officials in Justice's Office of Information Policy refer to this as the human readable report.) Beginning with fiscal year 2010, Justice required agencies to submit an electronic (i.e., machine readable) version of their annual FOIA report in a uniform open format to facilitate populating FOIA.gov. The two versions of the annual report are expected to be consistent.

16

Appendix I: Briefing for Staff Members of the
Committee on Oversight and Government
Reform, House of Representatives

FOIA.gov data, which are from the machine readable versions of agencies' annual reports, were generally consistent (i.e., complete and accurate) representations of agencies' fiscal year 2010 human readable annual reports. For fiscal year 2010, FOIA.gov includes data for all 97 of the agencies that were required to submit an annual report. Our comparison of 240 data elements between FOIA.gov and the agencies' human readable reports identified two discrepancies. According to Justice, the data in FOIA.gov were correct but the discrepancies resulted from typographical errors in the human readable versions of two agencies' annual reports.[12] Specifically,

- The Equal Employment Opportunity Commission's number of denied requests that were completely reversed or remanded on appeal was correctly reported on FOIA.gov as 56, while the agency's annual report erroneously stated 560.

- NARA's total number of FOIA staff was correctly reported on FOIA.gov as 25, while the agency's annual report erroneously stated 0.

As of April 2012, the agencies had corrected their annual reports, based on our identification of these discrepancies.

---

[12] We identified four additional discrepancies where FOIA.gov and agency annual reports differed by less than 0.68 percent.

17

Appendix I: Briefing for Staff Members of the
Committee on Oversight and Government
Reform, House of Representatives

Results
Objective 1

According to officials in the Office of Information Policy, each agency is responsible for the data provided in its FOIA annual reports. Further, the department has taken steps to improve the accuracy and consistency of the data. These steps include providing annual training to agency personnel who are responsible for preparation of the FOIA annual reports and posting guidance for report completion and submission on the Office of Information Policy website. In addition, the department has implemented checks to ensure data consistency between the two report versions. Specifically, it has developed and provided agencies with a spreadsheet-based tool for creating the machine readable versions of their annual reports. The tool contains features that assist agencies in compiling their data and math checks to help ensure consistency.[13] While Justice officials also have a checklist they use as a guide to spot check the consistency of machine readable versions of agencies' annual reports against the human readable versions, the officials said the Office of Information Policy does not have the time or staff to check all the data.

---

[13]According to Justice's 2012 Open Government Plan, the department plans to enhance this tool so that it will generate both fiscal year 2013 report versions based on single data entry.

18

Appendix I: Briefing for Staff Members of the
Committee on Oversight and Government
Reform, House of Representatives

Results
Objective 1

<u>FOIA.gov's "Advanced Reporting" Feature Did Not Always Provide Complete Results</u>

FOIA.gov's "Advanced Reporting" feature provides users with the capability to generate custom reports based on user-selected queries. For example, users can create a report by selecting queries for "Requests" at "All Agencies" for fiscal year 2010. Justice is responsible for ensuring that this feature performs as intended (i.e., produces reports that are complete).

Our creation of reports using the "Advanced Reporting" feature produced results that were incomplete. The following are examples of the incomplete results that we found.

- A query on "Ten Oldest Requests" for all agencies for fiscal year 2010 yielded results for 82 agencies, with 15 agencies not shown.

- A query on "Ten Oldest Appeals" for all agencies for fiscal year 2010 yielded results for 43 agencies, with 54 agencies not shown.

- A query on "Exemptions" for Department of Defense components for fiscal years 2008 through 2010 yielded results for 91 components, with 3 components not shown.

- A query on "Backlog" for all agencies for fiscal year 2010 yielded results for 94 agencies, with 3 agencies not shown.

19

Appendix I: Briefing for Staff Members of the
Committee on Oversight and Government
Reform, House of Representatives

 **G A O**
Accountability · Integrity · Reliability

Results
Objective 1

- A query on "Response Time" for all agencies for fiscal year 2010 yielded results for 96 agencies, with 1 agency not shown.

- A query on "Requests Granted" for all agencies for fiscal year 2010 yielded results for 94 agencies, with 3 agencies not shown.

In March 2012, we discussed these incomplete reports with the Director of the Office of Information Policy and an official from Justice's Chief Information Officer's staff. They agreed to investigate the incomplete reports we called to their attention.

In April 2012, Justice provided explanations for the incomplete reports we identified. For example, a frequently cited explanation for incomplete reports was that FOIA.gov was not displaying agencies that did not have data to report. Justice provided documentation stating that the department had resolved the incomplete reports we identified.

Nevertheless, our experience using FOIA.gov raises concern about whether the "Advanced Reporting" capability will produce complete reports in response to all queries.

20

Appendix I: Briefing for Staff Members of the
Committee on Oversight and Government
Reform, House of Representatives

Justice has Made Improvements to FOIA.gov; Other Agencies Plan to Implement Complementary, Multiagency Capabilities

According to Justice officials, improvements to FOIA.gov are made as they identify needs or in response to users' feedback. The officials told us that the department had improved usability and navigation in July 2011. During the course of our review, Justice made, and we noted, additional improvements. For example, the department

- in December 2011, added a new search feature that allows users to locate information on agencies' websites, including records released in response to previous FOIA requests and documents that agencies have proactively disclosed; and

- in March 2012, added information in the Spanish language and added links to agencies' FOIA web portals.

21

Appendix I: Briefing for Staff Members of the
Committee on Oversight and Government
Reform, House of Representatives

 **G A O**
Accountability • Integrity • Reliability

Results
Objective 2

According to the Director of the Office of Information Policy, FOIA.gov was not intended as an internal FOIA processing system for federal agencies. Such systems generally include capabilities for agencies to track requests internally, provide tools for processing requests, and collect data for agencies' annual FOIA reports. In addition, these systems may include capabilities that allow the public to make requests online, track the status of their requests, and correspond with agencies regarding their requests. Three agencies, namely, EPA, Commerce, and NARA are currently engaged in a project to develop a FOIA processing system for use by multiple agencies. In particular, they are working jointly to develop a multiagency FOIA web portal, also referred to as the FOIA module, that is aimed at providing a system to assign and process requests, post responses online, and provide annual report information to Justice.[14] Further, the portal is intended to be used by the public to submit and track FOIA requests and to search and view results. Officials from EPA stated that the agencies intend to include an online "reading room" that contains information released as a result of FOIA requests made through the portal. These capabilities are planned to be deployed by the beginning of October 2012. According to EPA, Commerce, and NARA officials, the multiagency web portal is designed to complement the FOIA.gov website and they are open to collaborating with other federal agencies on this initiative.

---

[14] According to official's, EPA is responsible for the actual development of the portal because it will leverage the structure of its Regulations.gov website. Regulations.gov is an official online comment system and serves as a clearinghouse for materials related to agencies' rulemakings. NARA and Commerce are partners that are providing funding for the effort.

22

Appendix I: Briefing for Staff Members of the
Committee on Oversight and Government
Reform, House of Representatives

Conclusions

As intended, the FOIA.gov website is populated with data that originate in the FOIA annual reports that federal agencies are required to submit to Justice. While these data for fiscal year 2010 are generally consistent with those presented in agencies' published annual reports, the website's feature that provides users with the capability to generate customized reports was not reliable because it did not always provide complete results.

Justice has made improvements to enhance FOIA.gov, including the addition of a governmentwide search feature; however, it does not intend for the website to include capabilities that agencies would use to support management of their FOIA processes (e.g., processing FOIA requests). The Environmental Protection Agency, Department of Commerce, and National Archives and Records Administration are currently engaged in a project to develop a multiagency system that is intended to compliment FOIA.gov and provide such capabilities.

23

Appendix I: Briefing for Staff Members of the
Committee on Oversight and Government
Reform, House of Representatives

Recommendation for Executive Action

To ensure the reliability of reports generated from the "Advanced Reporting" feature of the Department of Justice's website, FOIA.gov, we recommend that the Director of the Office of Information Policy, in conjunction with the department's Chief Information Officer, make certain that the website's "Advanced Reporting" feature produces complete reports in response to all queries.

24

Agency Comments and Our Evaluation

An Attorney-Advisor in the Department of Justice, Office of Information Policy submitted written technical comments on a draft of this briefing via email. We have addressed each comment as appropriate. Justice did not provide comments on our conclusions or recommendation.

25

Appendix II: Department of Justice

U.S. Department of Justice

Office of Information Policy

Suite 11050
1425 New York Avenue, NW
Washington, DC 20530-0001

Telephone: (202) 514-3642

JUN 21 2012

Ms. Valerie C. Melvin
Director
Information Management and Technology Resources Issues
Government Accountability Office
Washington, D.C. 20548

Dear Ms. Melvin:

Thank you for the opportunity to review and comment on the draft Government Accountability Office (GAO) report entitled, "Freedom of Information Act: Key Website Is Generally Reliable, but Action Is Needed to Ensure Completeness of Its Reports." The Department of Justice appreciates GAO's work in planning and conducting this review and issuing the report.

We have completed our review of the draft report and our response to the Recommendation for Executive Action is as follows:

> **Recommendation:** To ensure the reliability of reports generated from the "Advanced Reporting" feature of the Department of Justice's website, FOIA.gov, we recommend that the Director of the Office of Information Policy, in conjunction with the Department's Chief Information Officer, make certain that the website's "Advanced Reporting" feature produces complete reports in response to all queries.

> **Response:** OIP agrees with GAO's recommendation, but respectfully notes that during GAO's audit, the Department's Office of the Chief Information Officer (OCIO) developed a comprehensive solution to resolve the issue of some agencies and components of agencies not appearing in certain reports generated by FOIA.gov's advanced reporting feature. The Department believes that the OCIO's solution resolved all issues that would cause an agency or component not to appear in an advanced report. Nevertheless, OIP, in conjunction with the OCIO, will perform additional testing to re-confirm that FOIA.gov's advanced reporting feature is producing complete reports. The OCIO will retest the advanced reporting feature from a technical standpoint and OIP will conduct an additional review from a user's perspective. If any issues arise during this testing, the Department will take the appropriate measures to address them.

Additionally, OIP would like to clarify that although GAO's conclusion notes that the Department does not intend for FOIA.gov to serve as an internal FOIA processing system that would manage an agency's FOIA requests, FOIA.gov has a number of features that assist

- 2 -

agencies in their management of FOIA. By displaying graphically all the data contained in agency Annual FOIA Reports, agencies can use FOIA.gov to compare and contrast their own progress on multiple metrics over time and also against other similarly-sized agencies. For example, agencies can readily assess trends occurring in their administration of the FOIA, including whether they face increasing numbers of incoming requests and if they are meeting that demand without sacrificing timely responses to requesters. By analyzing the detailed breakdown of their processing times, agencies can also determine what, if any, improvements need to be made in the time it takes to respond to simple, complex or expedited requests.

Furthermore, FOIA.gov's new "Find" feature allows agencies to search for information located anywhere on any federal government website, which is particularly helpful when an agency is trying to determine whether information responsive to a FOIA request is already available on one of its websites or if it should direct the requester to another agency that is likely to have responsive records. The Department also recently added to FOIA.gov links to all existing agency FOIA request portals that provide online request-making capabilities such as allowing requesters to submit their FOIA requests or administrative appeals online. Currently, over 120 agencies provide such online capabilities that can be accessed through FOIA.gov. Moving forward, the Department is constantly exploring and planning for ways to further improve FOIA.gov to do even more to meet both the public's and agencies' FOIA needs.

Please do not hesitate to contact me if you have any questions regarding this response.

Sincerely,

Melanie Ann Pustay

Melanie Ann Pustay
Director

Appendix III: Department of Commerce

UNITED STATES DEPARTMENT OF COMMERCE
Chief Financial Officer
Assistant Secretary for Administration
Washington, D.C. 20230

Ms. Valerie C. Melvin
Director, Information Management and
   Technology Resources Issues
Government Accountability Office
441 G Street, N.W.
Washington, D.C. 20548

Dear Ms. Melvin:

Thank you for the opportunity to review the draft of GAO-12-754 – Freedom of Information Act: Key Website is Generally Reliable, but Action Is Needed to Ensure Completeness of Its Reports.

The Department of Commerce concurs that the FOIA Module/Portal is different from, but complimentary to, FOIA.gov. The multi-agency FOIA Module/Portal offers a cost effective and efficient solution for improved tracking and reporting and provides the public access to government documents.

The FOIA Module/Portal will enable agencies to provide reporting data to FOIA.gov and allows requesters to submit requests to a single government website, track the status of requests, and find, view, and download FOIA requests and agency responses. Building on the inherent capabilities for tracking, the FOIA Module/Portal will allow agencies to collect metrics that have not previously been available in a cost effective manner. The capability to collect these metrics will allow agencies to enhance their review of processes to increase efficiencies and economies of scale through ongoing/continual reviews and to update them as needed.

Again, we appreciate the opportunity to comment on GAO's draft report. If you have any questions regarding our comments, please contact Joey Hutcherson, Deputy Director for Open Government, at 202-482-0873.

Sincerely,

Scott Quehl
Chief Financial Officer and
   Assistant Secretary for Administration

NATIONAL
ARCHIVES

Via email

JUN 21 2012

Valerie C. Melvin
Director, Information Management and Technology Resources Issues
United States Government Accountability Office
44 G Street, NW
Washington, DC 20548

Dear Ms. Melvin,

Thank you for the opportunity to review and comment on draft report GAO-12-754, *Freedom of Information Act: Key Website is Generally Reliable, but Action is needed to Ensure Completeness of its Reports.*

We appreciate GAO's looking into FOIA.gov and the data that are available through that web site for analysis of agency FOIA activities. The accuracy and completeness of those data are very important to OGIS and throughout the FOIA community. We also appreciate GAO's recognition that the FOIA.gov web site is not intended as an internal FOIA processing system, as will be the multi-agency system that is being built by the Environmental Protection Agency in partnership with NARA and the Department of Commerce.

If you have questions regarding this information, please contact Mary Drak by email at mary.drak@nara.gov or by phone at 301-837-1668.

David S. Ferriero
Archivist of the United States

NATIONAL ARCHIVES *and*
RECORDS ADMINISTRATION
8601 ADELPHI ROAD
COLLEGE PARK, MD 20740-6001
www.archives.gov

Appendix V: GAO Contact & Staff Acknowledgments

GAO Contact	Valerie C. Melvin, (202) 512-6304 or melvinv@gao.gov
Staff Acknowledgments	In addition to the contact named above, Mark Bird (Assistant Director), Elena Epps, Nancy Glover, Jacqueline Mai, and Christy Tyson made key contributions to this report.